THE OFFICIAL
boyzone
POSTER BOOK

First published in 1998 by Virgin Books
an imprint of Virgin Publishing Ltd
Thames Wharf Studios
Rainville Road
London W6 9HT

A catalogue record for this book is available from the British Library

ISBN: 07535 0229 1

Printed and bound in Italy

Designed by Slatter-Anderson

Colour reproduction: Colourwise Ltd

ACKNOWLEDGEMENTS
My thanks to Ronan, Stephen, Shane, Keith and Mikey for their co-operation in the production of this book, despite their busy schedule. Thanks also to Boyzone co-managers Louis Walsh and John Reynolds and photographer Philip Ollerenshaw.

THE OFFICIAL
boyzone
POSTER BOOK

Eddie Rowley

Virgin

How ya,

Well, 1998 has been another exciting year for us here in Boyzone.

As you will discover by reading this special book, it's been non-stop action for all of us since January.

Our manager, Louis Walsh, seems to have forgotten that he promised us more time off this year!

But we're not complaining because already it's proving to be the best year of Boyzone's career.

We've got a new album out, a tour on the way and a greatest hits collection being prepared for Christmas. In between, as you will see from our profiles, we've also found some time to have some fun in our personal lives.

Highlights away from the stage included two marriages and Ronan's 21st birthday. And we've also picked up a few more awards along the way.

Thanks to you, the fans, we're still growing and developing as a band.

The next show is going to be spectacular and you can read more about that in this book.

We hope you enjoy this special souvenir of Boyzone and perhaps through reading it you'll get to know us even better. There are lots of facts and gossip, plus great posters and pictures from our collection.

1998 has been another great chapter in the career of Boyzone. Stick with us, and there'll be many more to come.

God bless from all the Boyz.

Mikey

He's idolized by millions of female fans around the world and enjoys wealth, fame and a jet-set lifestyle.

But these days, what gives Boyzone star Mikey Graham a real kick is... housekeeping! Ever since Mikey bought his dream home outside Dublin it's been his real passion. 'I just love going home to my house and working in it. I've become very domesticated. I know it's not very pop star-ish to say that, but at the end of the day you realize it's the simple things in life that really give you pleasure.'

- PLACE OF BIRTH
- **Dublin**
- DATE OF BIRTH
- **15 August 1972**
- STARSIGN
- **Leo**
- KEY CHARACTERISTICS
- **Confident, dominant, warm, loving and dynamic.**
- CHINESE HOROSCOPE
- **Born in the Year of the Rat. Charming, sociable and amusing.**
- HEIGHT
- **5' 8"**
- COLOUR OF EYES
- **Blue**
- WAIST
- **30**
- SHOE SIZE
- **8**
- STATUS
- **Dad to daughter Hannah.**

- PARENTS
- **Mum, Sheila, a homemaker. Dad Billy, a carpenter.**
- BROTHER
- **Niall**
- SISTERS
- **Yvonne, Avril, Cathy and twins Claire and Debbie.**
- EARLY ACHIEVEMENTS
- **Appeared in TV adverts for biscuits and the Irish electricity board.**
- BEST SCHOOL SUBJECTS
- **English and Art.**
- EARLY JOBS
- **A mechanic.**
- EARLY SHOWBIZ EXPERIENCE
- **Played in several Dublin bands, including one called Ivory.**

'I love our new album. The music we're making now is more mature and I'm feeling a lot more relaxed with it.'

Mikey's new home rings out with the laughter and joy of a toddler... his beautiful two-year-old daughter Hannah. Like all proud parents, Mikey and his girlfriend Sharon now live their lives around little Hannah.

He says: 'When you become a parent your whole world changes. You stop being selfish. What you do is not about you anymore, it's about this little person you've brought into the world.

'It's been tough for me since Hannah came along. There's the pain of separation when I have to go away for long periods with Boyzone and leave Hannah behind. No one knows what I've gone through deep inside.

'But Boyzone is what I do for a living. I love it. I love the reaction I get from the fans.'

Like all the lads in Boyzone, Mikey hasn't allowed fame or wealth to change him as a person.

'Being Irish, being natural, being normal, the fans like that about us.'

This year Mikey sponsored his local soccer club, Kilmore, and they proudly wear his name on their jerseys. He enjoys being part of a local community.

The star remains close to his family and he admits that one of the greatest joys the success of Boyzone has given him is the ability to take care of his parents.

'My parents gave me and the rest of the family a great childhood. There were seven of us and it wasn't easy. They had to make sacrifices along the way, now I can make sure that they'll never want for anything.'

The roar of the fans is sweet music to Mikey's ears when Boyzone are on tour. He loves his job and when you love something you're

doing, it's never work. He loves his music.

'Music is one channel where I can really express myself emotionally because I have a real problem showing my emotions. I find it hard to cry.

'I've written lots and lots of songs. They don't suit Boyzone's style so you won't be hearing them yet. They'll come after Boyzone, and hopefully that won't be for a long time yet.'

Boyzone has taken Mikey to some of the most interesting countries in the world. And along the way he has bumped into some people he personally admires and respects, among them his movie idol Robert de Niro.

Mikey says: 'Meeting Robert de Niro was a real thrill for me because I've been a lifelong fan. We met by chance in a hotel restaurant at breakfast one morning and I went up and introduced myself to him. He was charming. Although they have received many awards around the world, success at home is very important to Mikey.

'I love Ireland and I love Dublin and it's personally rewarding to be respected in your own country.

'This year we were voted Best Pop Act in the Heineken/Hot Press Rock Awards. I was really thrilled with that because it's a very prestigious award in our country. Hopefully there'll be lots more to come.'

Ronan

Ronan Keating has grown up in the spotlight.

He was a naive young lad of 16 when he joined Boyzone, and he has been moulded into a superstar through his experiences. But despite the pressure of his enormous fame, Ronan has retained his personal charm and friendly nature.

'I've always known that fame is very fickle. One minute the whole world loves you and then you're forgotten. It could happen to me and all the lads in Boyzone.'

- PLACE OF BIRTH
- **Dublin**
- DATE OF BIRTH
- **3 March 1977**
- STAR SIGN
- **Pisces**
- KEY CHARACTERISTICS
- **Sensitive, selfless, sympathetic, mystical and modest.**
- CHINESE HOROSCOPE
- **Born in the Year of the Snake. A serious thinker and a wise person.**
- HEIGHT
- **5' 9"**
- COLOUR OF EYES
- **Blue**
- WAIST
- **30/32**
- SHOE SIZE
- **9**
- STATUS
- **Married to Yvonne.**

- PARENTS
- **Gerry and the late Marie Keating.**
- BROTHERS
- **Ciaran, Gerard and Gary.**
- SISTER
- **Linda**
- EARLY ACHIEVEMENTS
- **A keen athlete, Ronan was an All Ireland champion runner.**
- BEST SCHOOL SUBJECTS
- **English, History and PE.**
- EARLY JOBS
- **Worked part-time in shoe shops while still at school.**
- EARLY SHOWBIZ EXPERIENCE
- **Ronan formed two rock groups before Boyzone. He was the singer and once won £1,000 in a talent contest.**

'You just know
when someone
comes along
that they are
right for you.
That's the way
I felt about
Yvonne.'

The youngest member of Boyzone has achieved more in five years than most people do in their lifetime.

But the sad star readily admits he would give it all up to have his beloved mother Marie back in his life. She lost her brave battle with cancer last February and Ronan's life changed utterly.

'I'm devastated. Mum was my best friend. I phoned her every day, no matter what part of the world I was in. What can I say, I miss her madly.'

Since then, Ronan has found happiness again by marrying his Irish model girlfriend Yvonne Connolly. The glamorous couple stunned the showbiz world with their surprise marriage on the Caribbean island of Nevis.

He says: 'Yvonne has made me so happy. We started out being friends and then I realized that I was in love with her. When I eventually told Yvonne luckily she felt the same way about me.

'I'm delighted with the way the fans have reacted. I know some are disappointed but they say they are glad that I'm happy and that means so much.'

It's also been the year when he officially entered Manzone, celebrating his 21st birthday on 3 March. That was a night to remember when his family, friends and showbiz pals joined him at a mega-bash in Dublin's Red Box club.

Ronan arrived at the club on his Harley Davidson, and there was a beautiful classic Ford Mustang car on the dancefloor to add to the atmosphere.

Car-mad Ronan instantly fell in love with it, and

Shane, Keith and Steve later presented him with the dream machine as their birthday gift. Just a couple of weeks later he got the chance to drive it in style when he was invited to be the Grand Marshal in Dublin's St Patrick's Day Parade.

'Words can't describe the feelings of pride I had as I led the parade. It's a day I'll always remember.'

The personal awards and nominations just kept on rolling in for Ronan this year. He was voted Britain's Spectacle Wearer of the Year, beating contenders that included Gary Barlow. But the one that made him most proud was the Ivor Novello award (the music industry's equivalent of an Oscar) for Best Song From a Movie for the Bean track and Boyzone hit, 'Picture Of You'. 'I still can't believe it,' he says.

Neither can he believe that stars like Elton John, Bono, George Michael and Gary Barlow hold him in such high esteem. Elton invited Ronan to his 50th birthday party last year, George Michael personally phoned to sympathize on the death of his Mum and Gary invited Ronan to duet with him at a Dublin show.

Ronan is hotly pursued by fans from Bristol to Bombay and there are often times when it gets scary as crowds swarm around him.

'I've been thrown to the ground and had my hair pulled. I don't wear an earring anymore. They get pulled off. I've had jackets and shirts ripped. It's madness at times.

'But I don't get angry at that. This is my life. I accept it and I live with it. I understand where the fans are coming from. I'm glad they're there. They're buying our records, videos and books. They are responsible for everything we have and I appreciate them.'

Keith

It's been a rollercoaster ride for gentle giant Keith Duffy since Boyzone became one of the world's biggest pop acts.

Like Mikey, he's had to juggle life as a dad with long stretches away from his native Dublin. The joy that Keith's little son Jordan has brought into his life is openly displayed. 'He's a great little fella and I hate going off and leaving him. I'm always afraid that he won't remember me when I return.'

PLACE OF BIRTH
Dublin
DATE OF BIRTH
1 October 1974
STARSIGN
Libra
KEY CHARACTERISTICS
Social, outgoing, charming. Likes those around him to be happy.
CHINESE HOROSCOPE
Born in the Year of the Tiger. Great energy and courage, very passionate and likes to be in charge.
HEIGHT
6' 1"
COLOUR OF EYES
Blue
WAIST
32
SHOE SIZE
11
STATUS
Dad to son Jordan.

PARENTS
Mum Pat, a hairdresser. Dad Sean works in a department store.
BROTHERS
Derek and John
SISTERS
None
EARLY ACHIEVEMENTS
An ace Irish footballer and hurler.
BEST SCHOOL SUBJECTS
Technical Drawing and Construction Studies.
EARLY JOBS
Working in a department store and clothes shop.
EARLY SHOWBIZ EXPERIENCE
Played drums as a child in his local marching band. Joined a Gothic band called This Burning Effigy at 18.

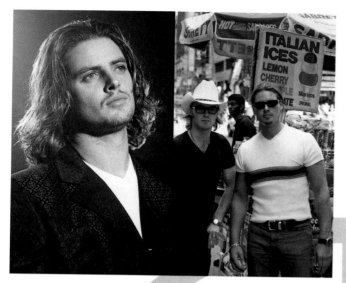

'Jordan's the best thing that ever happened to me. I cried my eyes out when he was born. I'd love to take him on tour with Boyzone. Maybe when he gets older.'

'It's been hard. Real hard. It may not have been obvious to the fans, but I've often been torn apart. It may have looked like a life of glamour and non-stop fun, but there have been lots of tears in private as well.'

'Don't get me wrong, I love Boyzone. I wouldn't change what has happened to me for the world. I've been dealt the lucky cards in life. I've got my dream, but a few nightmares came with it. Still, things are great now and I have nothing to complain about, thank God.'

Tall, dark and handsome Keith is the cheeky devil of the group. He's full of fun, a practical joker who is always the last one to bed when the Boyz are on tour.

'I know that Boyzone isn't going to be around forever, so I'm determined to enjoy it while it lasts.

'I don't want to miss anything and regret it later in life.'

'I know I've been luckier than a lot of people. I've been given the opportunity to travel the world and soak up different cultures. I hope it has made me a more interesting person, a wiser person.'

Keith admits he didn't have a lot of confidence or self-esteem when he first joined Boyzone. But that's all changed. Being exposed to adoration from the fans has helped him to become a stronger person. Keith was chosen for Boyzone after the band's manager Louis Walsh spotted him dancing in trendy Dublin nightclub The POD. But the star admits that in the early days he wasn't the best dancer or singer in the group. Five years down the line he's an accomplished performer who struts his stuff with style and panache.

'I feel good about myself in Boyzone now. I've got lots of confidence because I know that I perform well.'

'This year I even got the chance to go into the studio and do lead vocals on a few songs. They'll be turning up on the B-sides of singles or as additional tracks on an album.

'I've also co-written a song called 'Where Have You Been' with our co-producers Ray Hedges and Martin Brannigan. It'll turn up somewhere and, please God, the fans will like it. That's been a great new experience for me and hopefully I'll be doing some more in the future.'

His biggest fault these days, he admits, is spending money. 'I go through a horrendous amount of money. I just can't help myself. I'll fork out £280 on a shirt or pick up a really expensive mobile phone going through duty free in an airport, even though I have a perfectly good one. I hope my parents never find out, they'd kill me!'

Shane

The term 'cool' was invented for Shane Lynch.

Tell him that the world is about to end and he'll probably casually stroll out the door to take a final glance at the latest car in his life. 'Mr Unfazeable' has always given Boyzone an extra-special ingredient that's difficult to define. Perhaps it's his distinctive style – baggy trousers, gold chains and ever-changing hairstyles, as well as his trademark shaved eyebrow. It may be his general attitude – quietly confident and self-assured, yet friendly and approachable. Whatever it is, Shane has it... mountains of it.

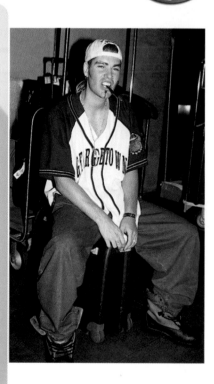

- PLACE OF BIRTH
- **Dublin**
- DATE OF BIRTH
- **3 July 1976**
- STARSIGN
- **Cancer**
- KEY CHARACTERISTICS
- **A homebird, sensitive, kind and compassionate.**
- CHINESE HOROSCOPE
- **Born in the Year of the Dragon. Refined, self-assured and unusual.**
- HEIGHT
- **6'**
- COLOUR OF EYES
- **Blue**
- WAIST
- **30**
- SHOE SIZE
- **9**
- STATUS
- **Married to Easther from Eternal.**

- PARENTS
- **Dad Brendan, a mechanic and mum Noeleen, a homemaker.**
- BROTHERS
- **None**
- SISTERS
- **Tara from girl band Fab!, Alison, twins Keavy and Edele from B*Witched and Naomi.**
- EARLY ACHIEVEMENTS
- **All Ireland BMX Champion and winner of the Portuguese BMX Championships.**
- BEST SCHOOL SUBJECTS
- **Irish (Gaelic), French and History.**
- EARLY JOBS
- **Worked as a mechanic.**
- EARLY SHOWBIZ EXPERIENCE
- **A dancer.**

'I always
knew I would
be rich and famous.
I said it to people. But it
wasn't just words. I KNEW
it was going to happen.'

Shane is the style guru of Boyzone. Fashion is an important feature of both his private and professional life.

He says: 'I've got a good sense of style. I think it's one of my strong qualities. I'm different. I know I am. Not in a big-headed way, but it's something that makes me feel good.

'I've never regarded myself as sexy, but stylish definitely.'

'I do think that's what I contribute to Boyzone. Ronan does the singing, Steve is the cute, smiley one and I'm the one with the image and it's not something that's false... it's me.'

There's never any fuss in Shane's life. Even his surprise marriage to Easther Bennett from Eternal was done without being turned into a showbiz circus. The couple wed in private at the magnificent 500-year-old Leez Priory near Chelmsford, Essex.

Outside of Boyzone, cars are his biggest passion. He even unashamedly rates them ahead of his family as the most important things in his life. Shane is obsessed with them. If he's not driving his latest sleek machine then he's engrossed in a car magazine.

Ask the other Boyz what he talks about most of the time and they'll tell you: 'Cars, cars, cars and more cars.'

Shane admits: 'There's nothing I like more than getting under the bonnet of a car and getting my hands dirty. It makes me feel really good at the end of the day.

'One of the best things about Boyzone's success is that I've been able to indulge my passion for cars by buying what I want.

'In the early days I missed my cars so much when I was away from home on tour with Boyzone that I used to take pictures of them with me. I know it's pretty sad, but that's how much I love cars.'

Ask Shane how he achieved his ambition, his dream, his fame and his wealth and he will say simply: 'Self-belief and a positive approach.'

While he started his working life as a mechanic, he knew instinctively that it wasn't going to be his ride through life.

'I knew I would do something else, but in my early teens I still hadn't decided what it would be. I always had a belief in myself. Watching the Smash Hits awards one year finally sparked off my dream. As I watched the bands perform I thought, "That's what I'd like to do." I knew then that I wanted to be in a band.'

Despite his love of fast cars and motor racing, it's surprising to find that Shane also enjoys more leisurely pursuits at his new home – like gardening!

'I love planting trees and shrubs and getting the garden organized. Believe it or not, it's a real pleasure. It doesn't compare with letting rip around a race track, but I do enjoy it.'

He's proud of his overall responsibility for Boyzone's choreography. And he's very professional. 'I have high standards,' Shane says, 'and I'm happy that Boyzone are now one of the best live acts around.

'I was really proud of our '97 stage show and the '98 tour is going to be outstanding.

'My ambitions for the future are simple – just to keep on producing more mindblowing shows and to make great music that thrills the fans. As long as we can do that, I'm happy.'

Steve

Few people in life are lucky enough to realize their most ambitious dreams.

Steve Gately is fortunate to have achieved all his – and more. The cute, smiley member of Boyzone readily admits he's had a charmed existence so far. Not only has Steve found pop superstardom, but he also got the opportunity to fulfil a personal childhood fantasy by working with the magical Disney corporation.

- PLACE OF BIRTH
- **Dublin**
- DATE OF BIRTH
- **17 March 1976**
- STARSIGN
- **Pisces**
- KEY CHARACTERISTICS
- **Sensitive, selfless, sympathetic, mystical and modest.**
- CHINESE HOROSCOPE
- **Born in the Year of the Dragon. Clever and bright, full of life, easy-going and attracts money.**
- HEIGHT
- **5' 7"**
- COLOUR OF EYES
- **Blue**
- WAIST
- **30**
- SHOE SIZE
- **7**

- STATUS
- **Single**
- PARENTS
- **Mum Margaret, a homemaker. Dad Martin, a painter and decorator.**
- BROTHERS
- **Mark, Alan and Tony**
- SISTER
- **Michelle**
- EARLY ACHIEVEMENTS
- **All Ireland Disco Dancing Champion at the age of 13.**
- BEST SCHOOL SUBJECTS
- **English, Science and Art.**
- EARLY JOBS
- **Worked as a barman in a local theatre.**
- EARLY SHOWBIZ EXPERIENCE
- **An extra in the movies *In The Name Of The Father* and *The Commitments*.**

'I'm too
soft for
my own
good.'

Despite his personal triumphs, Steve has no desire to jump the good ship Boyzone and go it alone in search of more solo glory.

'People are interested in us as a group. I don't know whether people would be interested if I did anything else.

'I try not to be negative about myself. I am determined to be positive and to push myself to do more and more. But I hate the thought of some day being without the other Boyz.'

Getting the call to perform his song 'Shooting Star' on the smash hit Disney movie *Hercules* has been one of the highlights of his career. He says: 'As a child, I loved anything from Disney and to think that I've worked with them is just amazing. I also got the chance this year to be a presenter for a day on the Disney channel, which was great fun.'

Steve, a huge fan of stage musicals, has also worked with Andrew Lloyd Webber. 'I performed a track on the CD of his musical, Whistle Down The Wind, and then I was invited to sing it at his 50th birthday party in London's Royal Albert Hall.'

Although he's not the youngest member of Boyzone – Ronan holds that distinction – he's treated as the baby of the group.

He has a very sensitive nature and is easily upset, so the other Boyz take care of him. 'They treat me like their little brother and they're very protective of me, which is nice. I know I take things to heart, but there doesn't seem to be a lot I can do about it.'

Although he's been to places he hadn't even heard of before Boyzone came along, Steve still insists his favourite country is Ireland.

He says: 'Ireland is home to me, so it's extra special. I've been all over the world and liked different countries for different reasons. France is great. I loved Australia. Some of the places we visited in Asia were amazing.

'But when it comes to settling down, I think Ireland will be my home. My family still live on the same street where I grew up and I love it there.'

Steve achieved another ambition this year when he passed his driving test and became the last member of Boyzone to enter the Carzone.

He says: 'Shanno and the other Boyz were always putting pressure on me to learn how to drive. Shanno used to say, "Steo, you don't know what you're missing, man. It's a great buzz. Learn to drive, man." So I did and now I drive a sporty Peugeot. And you know what? It is a great buzz!'

One of Steve's personal ambitions was to land a part in a movie and this year he was thrilled when he got the call to star in *The Mammy*, with Bette Midler and Angelica Huston.

He says: 'It's another great opportunity for me. The fact that it's a Disney film makes it even better. And I'm a big Bette Midler fan, so I couldn't have asked for anything more.

'Things just seem to get better and better for me all the time.'

'The work is hard, there's no denying that. But it's just a small price to pay for the fantastic life we lead. I'm really grateful to God for everything He has given me. I've been given more than I ever dreamed of. I just hope, with the backing of the fans, that Boyzone will go on and on. That's my new wish.'

Boyzone 1998 Tour

BOYZONE have been holed up in brainstorming sessions this summer in a bid to create the most explosive, innovative and mindblowing live show of their career.

Ronan, Steve, Shane, Mikey and Keith have got together in the BZ think-tank to bring you something extra-special for their 1998 autumn/winter tour.

Every year the Boyz step up a gear on stage with bigger and bigger extravaganzas. There's always lots of thrills, lots of eye-popping action, live music from the top backing band in the world and, of course, mesmerizing song and dance routines from the Boyz themselves.

The last Different Beat show cost half a million pounds to stage and it took five massive trucks to transport the mega-production from venue to venue. Eight dancers were brought in to give the show tons of energy and a different look. It involved months of preparation with lots of frenzied action behind the scenes.

The Boyz came up with their own ideas and these were combined with those from set designers and lighting experts. Judging by YOUR reaction, it was well worth the mammoth effort.

The question now is, can it get any better? The answer is a resounding...YES!

Ronan says: 'When you start off you don't have a lot of money, so you can only put on a show that's within your financial reach. The most exciting aspect of success is that it gives you the freedom to realize your dreams.

In our case, that means being able to devise and stage a show that is as thrilling for us as it is for the fans.

'I've seen some of the biggest and best shows in the world and thought, "Wow, I'd love to be able to do that." Five years down the road, Boyzone are now in that lucky position and we intend to make the most of it.

'We want something we're going to remember for the rest of our lives.'

And we want the fans to go "Wow!" when they see it.

'Our aim is to take you on a rollercoaster journey through singing, dancing and all kinds of other things. I can't really say much more because we want it to be a big surprise for all of our fans.'

'Everyone is going to be really surprised with the new show we've planned for the fans. We're pretty amazed ourselves. It's going to be very futuristic.'

The 1998 Boyzone show will feature each Boy performing a solo song for the first time, so we'll get a chance to hear what fantastic voices they all have.

Shane, who takes a personal interest in the choreography, has also dreamed up some special routines for himself and his palz.

Keith says: 'We want a show that will keep the fans totally focused on the stage because so much will be going on. I know it's going to

stretch us to the limits, which is good. We are really going out on a limb on this one.'

Mikey admits he can't believe just how big the Boyzone tour has grown over the years.

He says: 'We're so used to it now, but every now and then we have to stop and remind ourselves that it wasn't always like this.

'When we started out we played really small venues in Ireland and I remember one show where only ten people turned up. Mind you, we still went on and did the show.

'I'm really proud of the way Boyzone has matured. I wasn't 100 per cent happy with the band at the very start, but I am now. We've got a lot of respect in the business now, which is very rewarding.'

Stephen reveals that his favourite place on earth is under a spotlight out on a stage performing.

'I just love it,' he says. 'It's my favourite part of being in Boyzone because you get close to the fans and they give you all that love.'

 Mikey

To all the Fans,
                    Thanks very much For all
your tremendous Support and hope you'll keep it up.
                    You can do No Wrong in my eyes.
You built us up, day by day, week by week. month by month,
and year by year.
                    Boyzone just get bigger and bigger
and more and more people come along to support us.
These people were You!
                    Its true that we've worked hard for
our success. Nothing comes easy in life. But
without your tremendous support what Boyzone has
achieved would not have been possible.
                    You are the People who buy our
records, videos, books and everything else. When we go
on tour you are the ones who come out and
support us!
                    Personally its a great feeling to
get up on stage and experience the reaction we get
from you'll. You blow us away with all that excitement
and all that LOVE.
                    Please stay with us, thanks very
much.
                                    love
                                    from

Hello to everyone
I'd just like to say a big thank you
to ~~your~~ everyone from the bottom
of my heart

Words are not enough to say how
grateful I am to all of you.

What we have achieved in Boyzone
would not have been possible without
your support.

I hope that in return you have had some
joy and pleasure from what we do.

The only way we can repay you is by
staying more and more exciting shows
and recording songs that touch your hearts.

God Bless
From
Ronan

Keith

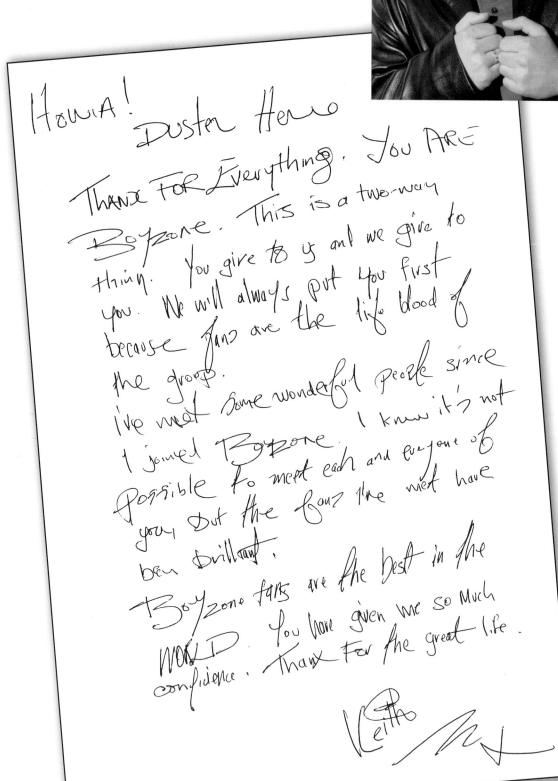

Howia! Duster Herro

Thanx For Everything. You Are Boyzone. This is a two-way thing. You give to y and we give to you. We will always put you first because Fans are the life blood of the group. I've met some wonderful people since I joined Boyzone. I know it's not possible to meet each and everyone of you but the fans I've met have been brilliant.

Boyzone fans are the best in the WORLD. You have given me so much confidence. Thanx for the great life.

Keith

Shane

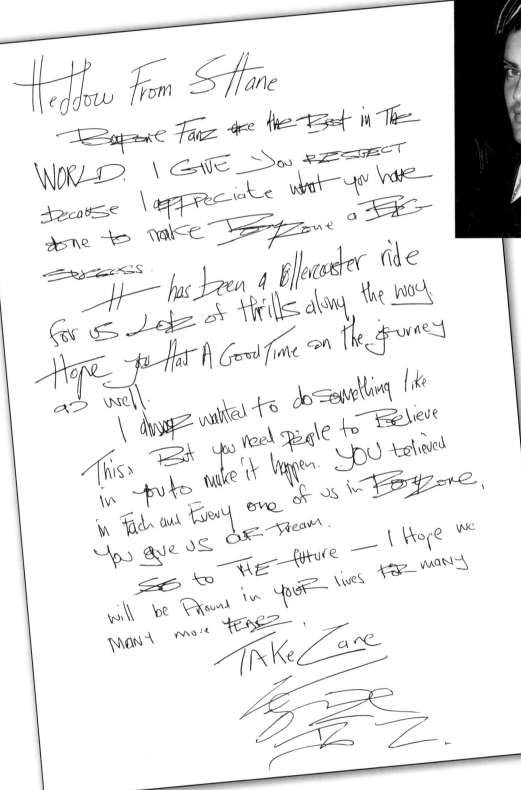

Heddow From Shane

Boyzone Fanz are the the Best in The
WORLD. I GIVE you RESPECT
because I appreciate what you have
done to make Boyzone a Big
success.

It has been a rollercoaster ride
for us Lot of thrills along the way.
Hope you Had A Good Time on the journey
as well.

I always wanted to do something like
This. But you need People to Believe
in you to make it happen. YOU believed
in Each and Every one of us in Boyzone.
You gave us our dream.

So to THE future — I Hope we
will be Around in your lives for many
MANY more years.

TAKe care

 **Steve**

Hi

Steve Here. I'd just like to say to
Everybody a million thanks for everything
and for making my life so Brilliant
You will always have a special place in my
heart.
You have followed us every step of the way
and encouraged us to aim higher and higher.
We couldn't have done it without you.
Whenever we had a moment of doubt
all we had to do was reach out to the
fans and you were there to boost us.
I love you all and try to personally
answer letters and cards. It's not always
easy, but I try because I know how
much it means to you.
I pray to God that you will always
be there for me as I will be for you.
Take Care + God Bless
✗ Steve